EVERYTHING
CHANGES

EVERYTHING
CHANGES

TEXT BY RUTH REA HOWELL

PHOTOGRAPHS BY ARLINE STRONG

ATHENEUM   1968   NEW YORK

To the small explorers who helped make this book.

Text copyright © 1968 by Ruth Rea Howell
Photographs copyright © 1968 by Arline Strong
All rights reserved
Library of Congress catalog card number 68-12238
Published simultaneously in Canada by
McClelland & Stewart Ltd.
Manufactured in the United States of America
Printed by Connecticut Printers, Inc.,
Hartford, Connecticut
Bound by H. Wolff, New York
First Edition

No CHILD is too young to study science. It is closer to his life than much of his usual schooling. The subject matter lies in his daily experience; the methods follow his own practice in exploring the world. No artificial tools of reading and writing need confuse him. Eyes, ears, fingers and an enquiring mind are the only prerequisites.

U. S. 1442432

LILLIAN PUTNAM
(from the *Shady Hill News*,
used by permission of the
Shady Hill School)

When school begins, it's fun to ride up and then down
again on a seesaw.

And talk to a friend on the playground.

You wear your summer clothes. The sand in the
sandbox feels warm on your hands and knees.

When the sun makes you feel very hot, you find a cool
place under the leafy branches of a tree to listen to
a story.

The tree makes a big shadow on the ground. No sunlight can shine through its leaves.

You make a shadow, too, when you climb between the sun and the ground.

When you take an exploring trip to the park, you look up and down and all around. There are so many trees and so many leaves on every branch, you can hardly see the sky.

Under a stone you may discover a millipede crawling on his many, many short legs.

On a rainy day you can wear your new raincoat to school and carry your new umbrella.

One drop and then another. It takes lots of raindrops to make a puddle.

Jack-o'-lanterns shine on Halloween.

By Halloween the weather feels cool and leaves are falling from almost every tree. Red leaves and chocolate colored leaves. Yellow ones and orange ones.

Now the fall time of year has begun.

You can make a pile of leaves to bounce and hide in.

When you go exploring in the park after Halloween,
you see the sky and the clouds. There are no more leaves
on the trees and no more leaf shadows on the ground.

Fall is the time to plant crocus bulbs. You push away the fallen leaves and dig down into the dark earth. There you find small sticks and stones and very old leaves and grass, all of them changing into earth soil. Dig your hole as deep as your hand from your wrist to the end of your longest finger.

Perhaps you will find a slippery worm.

Crocus bulbs look like little onions. They are planted
with the flat part at the bottom of the hole and the
pointed part pointing toward the sky. The bulb needs
two blankets, one of earth and the other of dry leaves.
Last of all, you stamp and tramp over the hole and the
two blankets so the crocus is tucked in tight.

In fall, flowers change into seeds. Some seeds have tops
as soft as a bunny's tail.

Some seeds have tiny hooks. A girl or a squirrel or a boy
or a dog could carry them a long way from where
they grew.

Some seeds jump off their stems when you touch them.

Seeds don't always fall near the plant where they grew.
Some seeds fly.

Trees have seeds, too. Some have wings like a bird or an airplane. Some have a prickly round cover.

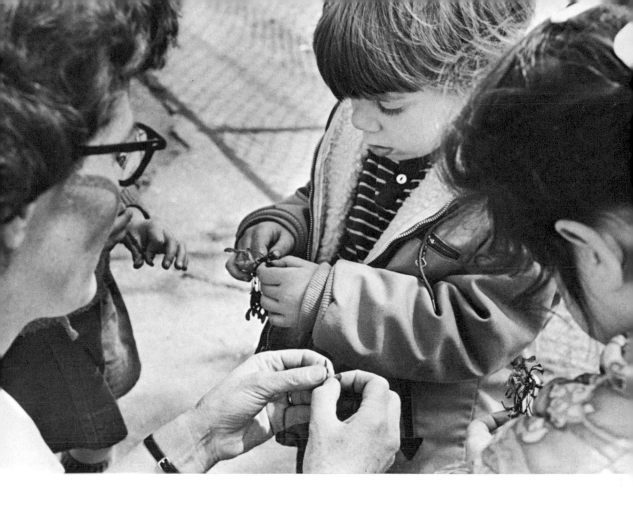

When you shake the cover you can tell how tiny the seeds are inside. All the seeds are ready to start changing into new flowers and new trees.

After all the leaves have fallen from their branches, the trees seem dead. But there is a bump on the end of each branch. The bumps have a tight cover. They are the tree's buds. In fall no more leaves come. Trees stop growing and wait. Buds wait and seeds wait.

By the month of November, it's hard work getting
ready to go outdoors.

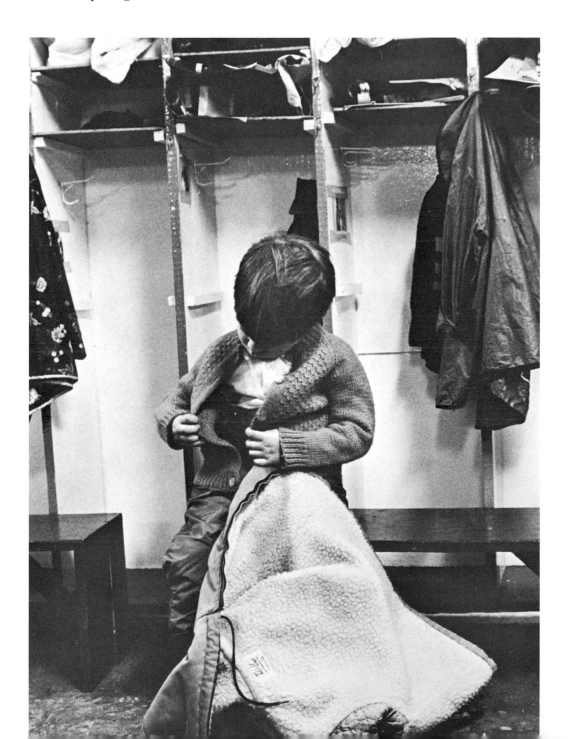

Because the mornings are colder, the parked cars may look white when you go to school. The white frost feels cold when you draw on it with your finger.

Perhaps you will find frost on a fallen leaf.

When you look at frost through a magnifying glass,
you can see it is made of tiny ice crystals like stars.

Now the sun does not shine long enough each day to make the weather warm. A new time of year has begun. Winter. There is a new blanket over the crocuses.

On a snowy day you can slide downhill.

You can make snow angels.

And tracks.

The winter cold freezes puddles. You can pick up a puddle when it turns to ice.

On a very sunny winter day, the snow melts and drips down. At night it freezes again. The drip has changed into an icicle.

On very sunny winter days the icy puddles melt and birds come for a drink. But it's hard for them to find enough to eat.

You can make a bird feeder out of two pie pans, and an empty juice can, two pieces of wood and a wire.

Join them all together. Make small holes near the
bottom of the can and fill it with bird seeds.

Fasten the feeder to the playground fence and stand
quietly and watch.

After Valentine's day comes the "lion" and "lamb"
month of March. Lion days are cold. The wind roars
like a lion. Lamb days are sunny. The breeze feels
as soft as a woolly lamb. On a lamb day the snow
blanket melts. Now you can push away the leaf blanket
where you planted the crocuses.

You can even dig
up one crocus and
look to see what
is growing on the
bottom. Then you
can plant it again.

Ladybug beetles come out from their winter hiding places on a sunny, lamb day. You may find one walking along the playground on her six legs. If you touch her she will fly away home.

All winter long worms waited under the frozen earth and leaves and snow, but now they are growing and wiggling again.

Even if snow falls one more time on a lion day, the crocuses will grow, because more days are warm than cold now. The crocus flower has pushed up through all its blankets. Spring is beginning.

All winter long buds waited to grow. Now they are soft and swelling.

Baby leaves and flowers are pushing their bud jackets off.

Tree buds have changed into tiny red and green flowers.

Seeds have grown into flowers, blooming in the grass.
You can pick a few and roll there, too.

Birds build their nests in spring. Robins look for
a safe place on a high up fire escape or a tree with thick
branches. Mother robin makes the inside of the nest
curved and smooth to fit her round red breast. She
lays her eggs, and sits very still, waiting for her babies
to hatch out of the eggs.

Sh-h don't frighten her.

Here comes a daddy to feed his hungry babies a
wriggling worm.

In spring inchworms hatch from their eggs on the bark of a tree.

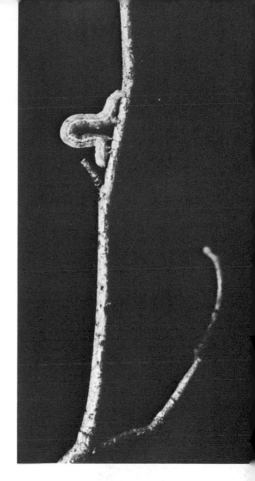

You may find an inchworm on a folded-over leaf. He makes it fold when he spins his web house inside.

The inchworm's legs are short and tickly.

While you are playing under a tree in spring, an inch-worm may let himself down on the thread he can spin.

In spring a bee finds something sweet in each flower.
Don't interrupt him.

Ants live in cracks in the playground pavement. They are hurrying to build their hill houses from the sandy dirt in the crack.

School is nearly over and spring is over, too.
It is light outside at supper time. Days are long and
warm, and nights are short. June comes and summer
begins. Time for cool clothes and a jump on a stump.

The big turtle loves a summer sunbath.

Guinea pigs like summer shade and green
tree leaves to eat.

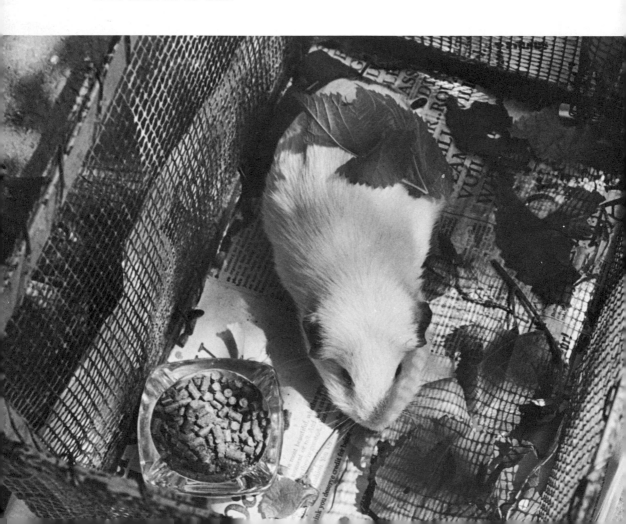

The way to keep cool is to jump in a pool.

Or you can look for a shady story tree just as you did when school began. The tree has changed many times while you were going to school. Do you remember what happened to its leaves in fall and how it looked in winter? In spring do you remember its flowers and pale green baby leaves? Now those leaves are big and dark, dark green. And all year long, you have been growing and changing, too.